# THE
# WRIGHT BROTHERS
# STORY

1911 Wright B replica. Students learned to fly in this model at the Wright Flying School. (Courtesy of National Park Service)

# THE
# WRIGHT
# BROTHERS
# STORY

## MIKE ROUSSEL

The
History
Press

First published 2017

The History Press
The Mill, Brimscombe Port
Stroud, Gloucestershire, GL5 2QG
www.thehistorypress.co.uk

British Library Cataloguing in Publication Data.
A catalogue record for this book is available from the British Library.

ISBN 978 0 7509 7047 1

Typesetting and origination by The History Press
Printed in Turkey

*Cover illustrations: Front:* The first successful
flight of the flyer on 17 December 1903.
*Back:* Group photograph in front of the
glider at Kill Devil Hills in 1911.

# CONTENTS

**H**umans have long been fascinated by the flight of winged animals, but the first attempt to replicate their flight by building crude, flapping wing machines, known as ornithopters, was made during the late fifteenth century in Italy by Leonardo da Vinci, although his design was never built or tested. Other attempts continued through the sixteenth and seventeenth centuries, but all failed and crashed. Eventually, however, it was noticed that when birds descend they spread their tail wings, stall in the air and then land tail down – inspiring the idea of adding a tail to the existing flying machine.

From then on, a number of aviation inventors were successful in their endeavours to create an ornithopter capable of flight. During the eighteenth century Sir George Cayley discovered that the arched shape of a bird's wing was an important feature of bird flight, and so he created a similar shape for a fixed-wing aircraft. The pioneering work of Sir George Cayley was to become a source of inspiration for future aviators.

During the latter half of the nineteenth century, German engineer Otto Lilienthal built a type of hang glider and became the first man to launch himself into the air, fly for some distance and then land safely. Lilienthal went on to design and build a number of variations of the glider and achieved over 2,000 glider flights before he died in a glider crash in 1896.

French inventor Clément Ader designed a steam-powered monoplane with wings, influenced by the study of the wings of a bat in 1890. He named it Éole, and although it did achieve a powered take-off, the 'flight' only consisted of uncontrolled hopping just a few inches off the ground for a distance of 164ft, due to the machine being underpowered and its heavy weight.

Other significant contributions to the development of flight by the end of the nineteenth century included Samuel P. Langley's experiments with steam-powered model aircraft that he flew up the Potomac River in the USA, and the construction of gliders by Octave Chanute and his friend Albert Herring, which they flew along the shores of Lake Michigan in the USA. Chanute later became a great supporter of the efforts of the Wright brothers in their quest for what they believed would be the first powered, manned, heavier-than-air controlled flight. The Wright brothers would change the course of history when they achieved this milestone on 17 December 1903.

## CREDITS

All images sourced from Library of Congress unless otherwise stated. Catalogue numbers available on request.

Library of Congress www.loc.gov/collection/wilbur-and-orville-wright-papers
Library of Congress www.loc.gov/pictures/collection/wri
Edward Roach, Historian, Dayton Aviation Heritage National Historical Park
The Collection of The Henry Ford. Gift of Ford Motor Company
Images courtesy of Library of Congress Prints and Photographs Division, Washington, DC 20540 USA

**R**everend Milton Wright married Susan Catherine Koerner on 24 November 1859 and they had five children together: Reuchlin, born 1861; Lorin, 1862; Wilbur, 1867; Orville, 1871; and Katharine, their only daughter, born in 1874.

Reuchlin and Lorin both married and lived in Kansas, but while Reuchlin remained in Kansas, where he raised cattle, Lorin moved back to Dayton to become a bookkeeper. Wilbur and Orville famously remained bachelors. Their sister Katharine married an old college friend, Henry J. Haskell, on 20 November 1926, but she died in 1929 after contracting pneumonia.

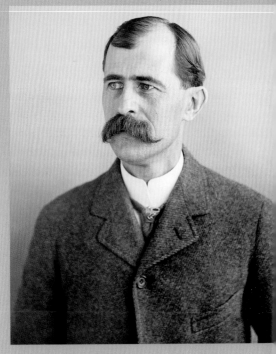

⌃ Wilbur and Orville's elder brother Reuchlin, aged 40.

Wilbur was born on a farm near Milville, Indiana, but two years later the family moved to 7 Hawthorn Street, Dayton, Ohio, where Orville was born on 19 August 1871. In 1877 Milton was elected bishop and moved his family to Cedar Rapids, Iowa. One of Wilbur and Orville's earliest memories was a Penaud's toy helicopter their father gave them in 1878 after returning from a church business trip. They found it intriguing

︿ Orville, Katharine and Wilbur.

◂ Wilbur and Orville's other elder brother Lorin.

No. 7 Hawthorn Street, Dayton was the family home of the Wright's from 1871–1914.

that whenever the helicopter was tossed into the air it didn't crash back down, as they expected it to, but would flutter to the ground.

This was of great interest to the boys, and they played with it until it broke. Keen to replace the broken helicopter, they went about making their own, which they named 'bat'. This simple toy made of wood, and with rubber bands to turn the propeller, was the spark that ignited the boys' interest in flight and flying machines. From then on Wilbur took up kite flying and, as an avid

### DID YOU KNOW?
The first kites, called *muyuan* (wooden kite), were flown over 2,000 years ago in Shandong, China.

▲ Nine of the Ten Dayton Boys' Club. Lorin, seated far right, and Reuchlin and Wilbur standing second and third from left.

reader, was keen to absorb books and newspaper articles about the ongoing development of aviation. Although he was not at first as deeply interested as Wilbur, Orville still regularly accessed their father's extensive library and became more absorbed in aviation matters.

In 1881 the family moved once again, this time to Richmond, Indiana, where Milton became a circuit preacher in the Indiana churches, but, not long after this, Susan was struck with tuberculosis and the family moved back to Dayton. At the time, Wilbur was preparing for university, but after the move he changed his plans and left high school without graduating. Shortly after leaving, however, he sustained a serious sports injury and was no longer able to work, becoming a recluse and staying at home. Milton was away a lot on Church business and it was left to Wilbur to care for his mother until her death in 1889 at the age of 61. At that time Katharine was studying at Orberlin College, but after their mother died she took over the running of the household, later becoming a teacher at a Dayton high school.

While Wilbur stayed at home caring for his mother he became deeply engaged in reading and furthering his own education from his father's library. As his health started to improve he became the club secretary of the Ten Dayton Boys' Club, a gathering of past

◀ Wilbur working on a metal lathe in the bicycle shop.

school friends who met for social and athletic activities. Orville in the meantime dropped out of college and, with his friend Edwin H. Sines, started a printing business with a printing press he had acquired from his family. Later, he built a bigger press, which led to the creation of the Wright Bros., Job Printers business in 1888. The following year, Wilbur joined as a partner taking on the role of editor and they started printing the *West Side News*, which later became *The Evening Item*. This was followed by a weekly magazine called *Snapshots* in October 1894.

However, just two years previously, in 1892, the Wright brothers had noticed a surge of national interest in the pastime of bicycles and cycling and set up another business at 1005 West Third Street – the Wright Cycle Exchange, which changed to the Wright Cycle Company in 1894. The brothers eventually moved the printing business into the Hoover Block at 1042 West Third Street where

➤ Orville and Edwin H. Sines filing frames in the workshop.

they rented a second-floor suite at the front of the building. After a further two moves to other locations the brothers decided to combine the printing and bicycle business under one roof. This was to be their fourth move in 1895 to 22 South Williams Street, for which they paid $16 a month rent, and where they stayed until 1897 when they made their fifth and final move to 1127 West Third Street. In 1898 Edwin suffered an injury to his knee and was forced to give up the running of the printing business. The brothers decided that rather than employ another person to run the printing side of things, they would sell up and concentrate on their bicycle business and their investigations into flight.

⌃ Edwin H. Sines managed the Wright printing business while they were engaged on aviation matters.

**W**ilbur and Orville continued to work in the bicycle shop, where they gained valuable engineering experience from the manufacture of their own brand of bicycles, but their interest in aviation was further stimulated after they visited the aeronautical exhibit at the World Columbian Exposition in Chicago in 1893. Gradually their interest in flying machines and human flight became the overall focus of their life's work.

Wilbur had already been studying the work of Otto Lilienthal, Octave Chanute and Percy Pilcher, and on 30 May 1889 he wrote to the Smithsonian Institution affirming his belief that human flight was possible and asking for advice on study materials. An extract from Wilbur's letter shows the depth of thought and study he had already gone through:

I have been interested in the problem of mechanical and human flight ever since as a boy I constructed a number of bats of various sizes after the style of Cayley's and Penaud's machines. My observations since have only convinced me more that human flight is possible and practicable. It is only a question of knowledge and skill just as all aerobatic feats. Birds are the most perfectly trained gymnasts in the world and are specially well fitted for their work, and it may be that man will never equal them, but no one who has watched a bird chasing an insect or another bird can doubt that feats are performed which require three or four times the effort required in ordinary flight. I believe that simple flight at least is possible to man and that the experiments and investigations of a large number of independent workers will result in the accumulation of information and knowledge and skill which will finally lead to accomplished flight.

The Smithsonian Institute acted swiftly in response to Wilbur's letter and he received a package of pamphlets and articles in the post. The package included Louis-Pierre Moullard's 'Empire of the Air', Lilienthal's 'The Problem of Flying and Practical Experiments in Soaring', Langley's 'The Story of Experiments in Mechanical Flight' and E.F. Huffaker's 'On Soaring Flight'.

◀◀ The Webbert building that the brothers rented from 1897–1916 for their Wright Cycle Company before it was taken down and transported to Henry Ford's Greenfield village.

The Smithsonian Institute also suggested further reading to include Chanute's 'Progress in Flying Machines', Langley's 'Experiments in Aerodynamics' and James Howard Means' 'The Aeronautical Annual'. Wilbur got to work and studied all the material he had acquired from June to August and also decided to obtain Chanute's book and copies of 'The Aeronautical Annual' for 1895, 1896 and 1897, which were also recommended.

At first Wilbur turned, unsurprisingly, to nature to study birds in flight and went to the Miami River near Dayton to a place called the Pinnacles, where it was possible to observe the soaring of hawks and buzzards. He recorded in his diary that hawks were better at

soaring than buzzards, but would often resort to flapping because they needed greater speed. He also noted that damp days tended to be unsuitable for soaring unless there was a high wind, but no bird soared when it was calm. Further observations revealed that a bird would turn the forward edge of

◄◄ The Wright brothers' bicycle shop, now operated by the National Park Service as part of Dayton Aviation Heritage National Historical Park. This is the building the Wrights used from 1895–97, where their early studies into flight took place. (Courtesy of National Park Service)

## DID YOU KNOW?

**Leonardo da Vinci came up with the first flying machine design, inspired by the flight of winged animals.**

◄ Wilbur at the Pinnacles where he studied bird flight.

one wingtip up while turning the other wing down, causing the bird to turn right or left, and that when birds were in flight the tail was important for steering and helped to give stability, but when landing the tail feathers were spread out and pointed downwards. These observations were to help him in his studies into human flight and he came to the conclusion that there were three main areas to consider:

- A machine would require air flowing over the wings to give it lift
- A power plant to move it forward to a speed that would keep it in the air
- The means of controlling the aircraft when in the air

Wilbur considered what experimental approach he would use to test the balance of a machine in the air, being all too aware of the risks previous pioneers of human flight

## DID YOU KNOW?

In 1826, Bristol schoolteacher George Pocock developed the 'charvolant', a type of horseless carriage pulled by kites. It was claimed that speeds up to 20mph could be achieved.

had taken in testing their inventions – he would not risk his, or his brother's life, in possible unsafe flying machines.

In 1889 Wilbur made an interesting discovery while selling an inner tube to a customer in their bicycle shop. While talking to the customer, he noticed that he was twisting the alternate diagonal corners of the edges of the inner-tube box, which reminded him of birds twisting their wings to turn right or left while in flight. This led to the concept of wing warping, and that evening Wilbur returned home with great excitement and demonstrated what he had discovered to Orville, Katharine and her college friend Harriet Sillman.

Following on from what he had observed with the inner-tube box, Wilbur constructed a model made of split bamboo, paper and strings. After successfully testing the model, Wilbur began to build a biplane kite with a wingspan of 5ft, similar to designs Chanute used when making his first gliders.

The warping action of the wings would then be controlled by two lines from the kite to each of Wilbur's hands. By tipping the sticks forward the kite would lift up by the nose, and by pulling the sticks back the kite would dive. When the operator pushed one stick forward and pulled one stick back the kite would roll to one side, and by reversing the action the opposite roll would occur. This became known as 'wing warping'.

In an attempt to keep his idea secret Wilbur flew the first tests of the kite from a field to the west of Dayton, where the kite responded well to the warping of the wing surfaces to bank to the right or left. Three schoolboys had been watching him fly the kite, but after a strong gust of wind the kite suddenly darted towards the boys, who dived to the ground. Wilbur was able to maintain control of the kite, which flew over the boys, but this was a problem that he knew they would have to bear in mind in the future. Wilbur then went to camp Rain-in-the-Face, where Orville, Katharine and Harriet were on a camping trip.

of the results of the tests he had completed the week before.

The next step for the brothers was to experiment with a man-carrying glider that demanded specific engineer skills – not a problem for the brothers as they had already gained these skills through working in the bicycle shop. The brothers used their personal experiences to great effect, especially in incorporating what they had learned about balance and control from riding their bicycles. With regard to control, the brothers felt that it was necessary to consider the three axis of motion: roll, pitch and yaw. The roll axis was based on the wing-warping system, where the pilot was lying on the bottom wing with a foot-operated crossbar for warping the wings to bank left or right, or to bring the aircraft back to level flight. This system was later changed to the use of a hip cradle to warp the wings. For the pitch axis they decided to use an elevator

## DID YOU KNOW?

The only creatures capable of powered flight are insects, birds and bats, but flying fish can glide for some distance due to their large fins that act like wings.

positioned in front of the wings to control climb and descent, which was controlled by the pilot by a lever in his left hand. The yaw axis was developed on the 1902 glider, with a vertical rudder added at the

## DID YOU KNOW?

In 1871, Alphonse Pénaud was the first person to build and fly a heavier-than-air model flying machine that was powered by rubber bands. It was called the 'Planophore'.

rear of the machine to control the left and right motion of the nose of the aircraft.

Using the formulas used by Lilienthal and Chanute for calculating lift and drag, Wilbur was able to estimate the total weight of the craft, his own weight and the speed of the wind into which the glider would have to fly. An elevator was to be placed in the front of the wings, similar to the fixed surface on their 1899 kite.

In September 1899, just three months after Wilbur wrote to the Smithsonian Institute, the glider designs were ready, but from October 1899 their time would be taken up assembling the next year's stock of Wright's bicycles.

◄◄ Aviation pioneer Octave Chanute was a keen supporter of the Wright brothers.

## FIRST TRIP TO KITTY HAWK, 1900

Wilbur began to research the ideal sites for testing flying machines, and from his calculations he knew he would need somewhere with strong, steady winds and hills to practise gliding, and a soft surface such as sand for landing. He also considered that it was important to have a secluded site where they could work without being observed.

Wilbur wrote to Chanute on 13 May 1900 explaining his plans, mentioning that he and his brother had a bicycle business that would require their attention for at least nine months of the year, leaving just September to January when the shop was not as busy to undertake the experimental work. He also asked for Chanute's recommendation on possible sites. Chanute, always pleased to help any new enthusiast to human flight, replied swiftly, suggesting various options in Florida and California.

Wilbur also wrote to the United States Weather Bureau in Washington and was sent the monthly weather reviews for August and September. From his study of the reviews he discovered that Kitty Hawk, North Carolina, seemed to be a suitable location, but as Kitty Hawk was not familiar to him he wrote to Joseph J. Dosher at the Kitty Hawk Weather Bureau on 3 August 1900 for his advice. Dosher sent a reply on 16 August:

In reply to your letter of the 3rd I will say the beach here is about one mile wide, clear of trees or high hills and extends for sixty miles same condition. The wind blows mostly from the north and north east September and October which is mainly down this piece of land giving you many miles of sturdy wind with a free sweep.

He reminded Wilbur that it was not possible to rent a house there so he would have to bring tents. Dosher also sent a copy of Wilbur's letter to William Tate, the postmaster at Kitty Hawk, who was quite keen on the idea and was happy to offer as much help and support as was needed.

Wilbur wrote to Chanute on 10 August informing him that he intended to construct a full-size glider, with some of the work done at Dayton and some at Kitty Hawk. Wilbur informed his father that he would soon be travelling to the North Carolina coast to conduct experiments with his newly built flying machine and that Orville would be staying at the bicycle shop for a short time before joining him at Kitty Hawk. Lorin and Katharine were to manage the business while they were away.

On Thursday 6 September Wilbur travelled to Elizabeth City, North Carolina, and then on to the Outer Banks by boat. Once at Kitty Hawk, Wilbur met William

'Bill' Tate, who warmly welcomed him and invited him to stay with his family. For the next few days Wilbur started to assemble the glider, borrowing a sewing machine from Bill's wife to sew the sateen fabric on the wings.

Wilbur explained to Bill that they were looking for a suitable area to test their kites and gliders. The postmaster suggested to Wilbur that it would be good for Kitty Hawk if they set up camp nearby and recommended an area of sandy land with an 80ft hill situated in the centre. The wind conditions in the area were generally steady and between 10–20mph, due to the absence of trees that could affect the wind current.

Orville eventually arrived at the Tate's on Friday 28 September, bringing the tents and other supplies. The final touches to the machine were undertaken, and when completed the glider was a biplane with 17ft wings covered in cotton. The plan was to

◄◄ An elderly Captain William Tate and his wife standing in front of the original Kitty Hawk post office.

## DID YOU KNOW?

In 1901, Guglielmo Marconi used a hexagonal Levitor kite to transmit the first radio signals across the Atlantic – the kite line was used as the aerial.

➤ View of Kill Devil Hills at Kitty Hawk, North Carolina.

experiment with the pilot lying on the lower wing, using his feet on a T-bar to control the wing warping.

By Thursday 4 October the brothers had pitched their tent on the edge of the sand dunes about ½ a mile away from the Tate's and were supplied with a daily report from J. Dosher at the Kitty Hawk Weather Bureau. During their first tests Tom Tate, the 10-year-old son of Bill's half-brother Dan Tate, was the first to ride on the kite, as he was not too heavy, although as a safety precaution the brothers held two lines attached to the kite and made sure that Tom flew close to the ground.

But Wilbur was keen to attempt a flight. The plan was for Wilbur to stand inside a cut-out in the lower wing and hold on to the two inside lower ribs. Orville and

▽ The Wright brothers' first camp near Kitty Hawk.

⌄ Big Hill between Kitty Hawk and Kill Devil Hills. The wings of a glider can be seen at the top of the hill on the far right.

Bill were on the left and right of the craft, each holding a wingtip, plus about 15–20ft of coiled rope attached to the sides of the craft. Once Wilbur shouted he was ready the three men started to run into the wind until the craft lifted off, at which point Wilbur climbed aboard and lay face down with his feet in the T-bar and his hands on the elevator control. Very rapidly Wilbur started experiencing difficulties and became nervous, causing him to shout to Orville and Bill to pull him down. They responded quickly and pulled the craft gently down into the sand. Wilbur decided that it would be safer to undertake a few more flights with an unmanned kite, recording the results in his diary.

With the discovery that they would need a headwind of 25mph to get into the air, J. Dosher kindly loaned them a handheld anemometer to help them gauge the strength of the wind. During each of the first two days the test sessions lasted up to 4 hours, but after their first crash on the third day high winds made it impossible to do anymore flying; it was not until 10 October that the wind decreased to about 30mph. Further kite flying continued that morning using various chain weights, which Wilbur recorded very carefully in his diary, along with the wind speed and drag.

A tower was built at the top of the hill with a rope attached from the tower to the glider to test

> The 1900 Wright glider flying as a kite at Kitty Hawk.

the controls to the aircraft. With Wilbur aboard, Orville and Bill held the ropes attached to the wings and allowed the glider to achieve a height of 15ft – the height of the tower. They then loosened the ropes and the glider floated for a while, still being held by a rope attached to the tower. Wilbur was able to test the elevator and warping controls, but although he appeared to be able to use the controls he still felt something was wrong. After a few days of tests there was a sudden gust of wind while the glider was on the ground, which blew it over smashing all of one side; it took two days for repairs before they could return to testing. They had learned a very important lesson – not to fly the craft from a tower, something that Octave Chanute had already warned Wilbur about when they had been discussing his plans.

They returned to trials on 17 October to concentrate on testing in various winds and conditions, during which time the machine was flown while loaded

## DID YOU KNOW?

The world's first public flight was flown by Alberto Santos-Dumont on 12 November 1906. He flew 722ft in just over 21 seconds.

with weights of 25lb for the first tests and then 50lb of chain. The outcome of the trials revealed that the craft, when empty, would not fly in wind strength of less than 22mph. The unmanned tests gave the brothers a chance to investigate the control responses of a full-scale machine, but they found that when operating the craft from the ground it was not easy to control the wing-warping and rudder mechanisms at the same time.

Before the brothers had to return to Dayton on 23 October, Wilbur wanted at least one flight to enable him to experience what it was like in free flight; so, with Bill's help, they carried the glider the 3 miles to Kill Devil Hills where there was a dune with a gradual descent of about 100ft. When they got to the top of the dune they laid the glider down, facing the slope. Wilbur got aboard and lay down on the lower wing and signalled to Orville and William that he was ready. The two men started running down the slope while holding the wingtips and then let go. Wilbur flew a short distance at an altitude of about 5ft while increasing in speed until landing safely in the sand. After about twelve flights that day Wilbur was quite satisfied with the outcome and was ready to return to Dayton.

After the brothers had left, Bill's wife decided to cut the sateen from the wings to make dresses for her daughters – when the brothers returned in 1901 they only found the skeletal remains of the 1900 glider!

The Wright brothers had learned a lot while conducting trials at Kitty Hawk and were now fully aware of the conditions that they would experience when planning for future trials there, especially the heat and mosquitoes in the summer and the very cold weather of the winter.

## SECOND TRIP TO KITTY HAWK, 1901

Chanute had known the Wrights for barely six months when he discovered they had flown for the first time, but felt the need to warn them to be very careful about what they were doing. Wilbur was aware of the dangers and had promised his father that he would not take unnecessary risks and would look after Orville, an approach proven by the care he took over safety during the first trials. The correspondence between Chanute and the Wrights was considerable, with the brothers using him mainly as a sounding board.

From their previous experience at Kitty Hawk the brothers decided that it would be better to stay longer and planned a six-to-eight-week stay from September to October. They also decided to build a permanent camp at Kill Devil Hills, complete with a hangar to house the new glider. While back at Dayton the brothers had built a wind tunnel to test wing shapes and, along with

▲ The brothers rebuilding their glider in a wooden workshop. Their tent, which was used as living quarters, can be seen to the right.

their final calculations, the design of the new glider was completed by the middle of May 1901 – with a 22ft wingspan it would be the largest glider flown by the Wrights.

The brothers found they could leave earlier to go to Kitty Hawk because they were now able to employ an old friend and engineer,

Charles Taylor, to run the bicycle business while they were away. On arrival at Kitty Hawk they spent their first night at the Tate's before heading off the next day with their equipment to the Kill Devil Hills campsite.

Work started on the new hangar for the glider on 15 July and took them

<< Left to right: Octave Chanute, Orville and Edward C. Huffaker, with Wilbur standing.

< Wilbur lying on the bottom wing and controlling the glider in level flight in 1901.

> Wilbur lying on the bottom wing of the 1901 glider just after landing. The skid marks from previous landings can be seen in the sand.

three days to complete. Chanute's assistant, Charles Huffaker, arrived the following Thursday with a glider he intended to test and another of Chanute's assistants, a young George Spratt, arrived on 25 July (Spratt was well liked by the Wrights, but they were not so enthusiastic about Huffaker). Wilbur made seventeen successful glides on 27 July before he dived into the sand. In an attempt to shift the centre of gravity he tried various positions of the body, but there were still difficulties, so they decided to modify the glider to get rid of any defects.

On 5 August, Chanute arrived and Wilbur thanked him for all the publicity he had given to their work, not just in the USA but also in

▲ The Wright Cycle Company shop was their fourth bicycle shop location (1895–97). It was where the brothers started thinking about flight, and also where they were working when German engineer Otto Lilienthal died. (Courtesy of National Park Service)

> To the right of the red building there is an empty lot which was the location of the bicycle shop the brothers rented from 1897–1916. This is shown at the Dayton Aviation Heritage National Historical Park. Henry Ford purchased the bicycle shop in 1936, dismantled it and rebuilt it at Greenfield Village in Michigan. (Courtesy of National Park Service)

>> The 1902 glider flown as a kite by Dan Tate (left) and Wilbur (right) on 19 September.

Europe. Huffaker had already given up on the tests on his glider and told Chanute how impressed he was with the Wrights and their glider.

The outcome from the early glides demonstrated that Wilbur was able to fly a distance of 389ft after just a few flights. The Wrights left Kitty Hawk on 22 August with the problem of lateral control on their minds – Wilbur later confided that there was uncertainty as to whether or not they would ever resume their experiments. However, once back working in the bicycle shop, thoughts of giving up were soon forgotten and the brothers experimented with a test rig mounted on the handlebars of a bicycle for aerofoil tests. With the wind-tunnel tests the brothers were able to solve the problems of lift, air resistance and drag by designing a shaped wing that curved from front to back, and from that discovery they knew how they could develop their flying machines.

## THIRD TRIP TO KITTY HAWK, 1902

After leaving Dayton for Kitty Hawk, the brothers spent time repairing their 1901 glider and started work on the new 1902 machine, which was designed and constructed from the lessons learned on the previous machine. It was their biggest glider to date, with a wingspan of 32ft and two vertical tail fins for stability.

Up until this point Wilbur had been doing all the flying and had become quite proficient, but it was now time for Orville to start to learn. Due to some very difficult weather conditions his flights were delayed, but once the weather improved the flights continued, averaging

▲ Wilbur working in the shed at Kitty Hawk.

what they were doing and became friendly with Spratt, who arrived the next day. Chanute and Augustus Herring, who had built and tested a monoplane glider based on the work of Otto Lilienthal, came four days later during a rainstorm, causing some concern for the brothers as they would now have to somehow squeeze everyone into their sleeping quarters.

By 14 October everybody started to leave and on the way back Chanute managed to spend a few days with Samuel Langley. He explained the progress of the Wrights and encouraged Langley to go to the Outer Banks to see for himself. Although Langley telegraphed the Wrights to ask if

about twenty-five flights on good-weather days, with distances of over 500ft achieved.

Wilbur and Orville's brother Lorin arrived on 30 September to see

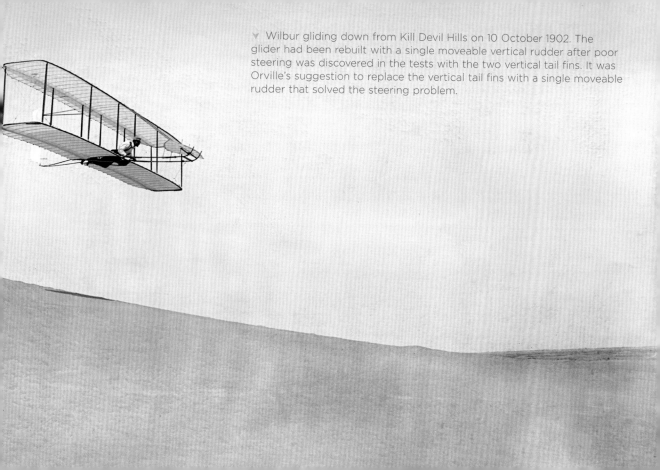

▼ Wilbur gliding down from Kill Devil Hills on 10 October 1902. The glider had been rebuilt with a single moveable vertical rudder after poor steering was discovered in the tests with the two vertical tail fins. It was Orville's suggestion to replace the vertical tail fins with a single moveable rudder that solved the steering problem.

⌃ The start of a glide in the 1902 glider. Orville is on the left, Dan Tate on the right and Wilbur is lying prone on the bottom wing.

≫ Wilbur, with Dan Tate running below.

he could visit, he was told that it was probably too late in the season to come.

Once Chanute and Herring had left, the brothers felt more relaxed and were airborne all day. They soon became quite proficient and were able to fly in any kind of weather; even with winds of about 30mph (the highest wind the aircraft had been gliding in) on 21 October they still brought the aircraft in to land without any trouble. On 23 October Wilbur set a record time for both time and distance when he completed a glide of 622.5ft in 26 seconds, with Orville making a very respectable glide of 615ft. They now held the record for the longest time in the air.

The Wright brothers were pleased with how well everything had gone and would have liked to continue flying, but had to leave on 28 October to catch the boat for Elizabeth City and then home, leaving their machines, including Chanute's, in the shed until they returned in 1903.

After returning to the bicycle business in November they worked on a new wind tunnel to measure the lift and drag figures. Wilbur also started writing to engine manufacturers, enquiring if they had an engine weighing 180lb that could power to 8–9hp, with the aim of adding power to their next machine; however, there were no positive responses so the brothers decided to design and make their own engine. With the help of their assistant Charles Taylor, who had experience working on engines, they had built their first engine in just six weeks. Next was to design a propeller, and after making their calculations the results were two 8ft, wooden propellers that they had shaped by hand. The engine would be connected by two large bicycle chains to twin contra-rotating propellers with a pusher configuration mounted behind the wings.

◄◄ Wilbur making his first right turn in a glider with the warp in the right wingtip close to the ground as he brings the wings level. It was the single moveable rudder that made this possible.

## FLYER I, KITTY HAWK, 1903

The Wright brothers left Dayton on 23 September, arriving at Kitty Hawk at midday on 26 September, only to be confronted with the job of repairing the damage caused by the winter storms. Dan Tate worked on constructing a new building to house the machines while the brothers transformed the older shelter into more comfortable living quarters. It was not until early the next week that they were able to get airborne in the 1902 glider, but once they could the brothers completed seventy-five glides on the first day alone.

The 1903 Flyer I was much larger, with a 40ft wingspan, a double horizontal front rudder and twin, moveable vertical rear rudders and two contra-rotating propellers. The flyer had to be strong enough to be able to carry a four-cylinder 12hp engine and with its increased weight it became impossible to attempt take-off from the top of the dune. To solve the problem of the extra weight the brothers built a 60ft launch rail, along which the machine would run and build up speed for take-off.

Orville had to return to Dayton on 8 December for machine parts, returning to Kitty three days later.

▲ One of four glides taken on 27 October 1903. Wilbur and Orville each made two glides.

Wilber standing in the doorway of the 1903 machine hanger on 24 November 1903. The living quarters were in the smaller wooden building to the right.

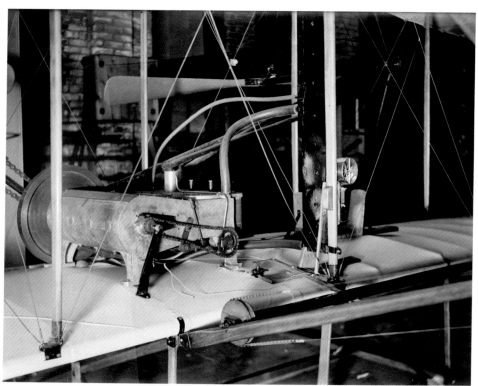

◄ The powered 1903 machine in the shop.

> The 1903 machine with its front wings for lift, engine for power, propellers for thrust and tail for stability.

>> Four crew members standing in front of the lifesaving station at Kill Devil Hills; John T. Daniels is second from the left. The crew helped the Wrights in their tests and also acted as witnesses to the first flights in 1903.

The machine was reassembled the following day, but for the next two days winds were too strong to attempt a flight.

On 14 December the weather was suitable for flying, so the brothers flew a large flag on the side of the hangar notifying the lifesavers that a flight was about to take

## DID YOU KNOW?

In 1903, American-born Samuel Cody was the first man to cross the English Channel in a canoe towed by kites.

place and that they would like their help. Bob Wescott, John Daniels, Tom Beacham, Will Dough, and Benny O'Neill visited the camp a few minutes later, along with some young boys who had been hanging around the station that morning. It was hard work moving the machine and placing it on the launch track, but all was ready by 2.40 p.m., and with the machine sitting on the rail they started the engine – the shock of the engine noise caused the boys to run away very quickly! Once the machine had warmed up, the brothers tossed a coin to see who was to make the first flight – Wilbur won. Orville recorded in his diary:

▼ The 1903 machine on the launching track for the 14 December trial. The four crew, with two small boys and a dog, are standing near the flyer.

Will started machine. I grabbed the upright the best I could and off we went. By the time we had reached the last quarter of the third rail, about 35 to 40 feet, the speed was so great I could stay with it no longer. I stopped and watch as the machine passed end of track. It had raised from the track six or eight feet from end. The machine turned up in front and rose to a height of about 15 feet from ground at a point somewhere in neighbourhood of 60 feet from end of track.

Orville recorded that the machine gradually sank and crashed in the sand, causing damage, so the next day was spent repairing the machine, which was completed by noon on 16 December. The brothers spent the afternoon with the machine set up on the rail waiting for the wind to pick up, but the conditions did not improve so they gave up for the day.

⊻ Wilbur in the damaged machine after the unsuccessful trial of 14 December 1903.

> Orville's diary entry of Thursday 17 December 1903.

Wilbur and Orville were up very early on the morning of 17 December and Orville noted in his diary:

> When we got up winds of between 20 and 25mph was blowing from the north. We got the machine out early and put out the signal for the men at the station.

Bob Wescott was on lookout duty in the lifesaving station that morning looking through his telescope for any ships in trouble and saw the flag flying on the wooden building. Promptly the lifesavers left, consisting of Adam Etheridge, John Daniels and Will Dough and accompanied by W.C. Brinkley of Manteo and Johnnie Moore of Nags Head.

By 10.30 a.m. the machine was set up on the launch rail and they started the engine. The brothers shook hands and Orville got on beside the engine with his feet braced against the board tacked to the rear spar. Orville wrote in his diary:

I got in the machine at 10.35 for the first trial. The wind, according to our anemometer as this time, was blowing a little over 20 miles per hour, 27 miles according to the movement of the anemometer at Kitty Hawk.

Wilbur asked John Daniels to look after the camera that was focused on the end of the rail. Orville comments in his diary:

The machine started off increasing in speed probably 7 to 8 mph. The machine lifted from the track just as it was in the fourth rail. Mr. Daniels took a picture just as it left the tracks.

The photograph would provide the necessary visual evidence to go with the witness statements of the five men to prove that the powered flight was successfully carried out. Later, Orville discovered that John Daniels had forgotten about the camera, but in his excitement at seeing Orville take-off it was thought that he had automatically squeezed the air bulb that tripped the shutter. Daniels admitted later that he could not recall if he had squeezed the

> The first
successful flight
of the flyer on
17 December 1903.
Orville is flying
the machine and
Wilbur can be seen
on the right. The
photograph was
taken by John T.
Daniels.

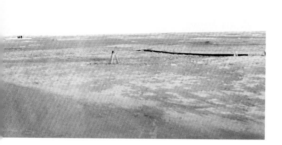

After repairs, at 20 mins after 11 o'clock Will made the second trial. The course was about like mine, up and down but a little longer over the ground though about the same time. Distance not measured but about 175 ft. Wind speed not quite as strong. With the aid of the station men present, we picked the machine up and carried it back to the starting ways. At about 20 minutes to 12 o'clock I made the third trial. While out about the same distance as Will's I met with a strong gust from the left which raised the left wing and sidled the machine off to the right in a lively manner. I immediately turned the rudder to bring the machine down and then worked the end control.

◄◄ Flyer I landing on the fourth flight of 17 December 1903 – it flew 825ft in 59 seconds.

bulb or not due to the excitement of the moment.

The machine left the rail and flew under its own power while under complete control of the pilot – the final time and distance was recorded as 120ft in 12 seconds. The brothers then got ready for the second trial and Orville records in his diary:

>> Close-up view of the damaged 1903 machine after the fourth and final flight on 17 December 1903.

Much to our surprise on reaching the ground the left wing struck first slowly the lateral control of this machine, much more effective than on any of our former ones. At the time of the sidling it had raised to a height of probably 12 to 14 feet.

At just 12 o'clock Will started on the fourth and last trip. The machine started off with its ups and downs as it had before, but by the time he had gone three or four hundred feet he had it under much better control, and was travelling on a fairly even course. It proceeded in this manner till it reached a small hummock out about 800 feet from the starting ways, when it began its pitching again and suddenly darted into the ground.

The front rudder frame was badly broken up, but the main frame suffered none at all. The distance was 852ft in 59 seconds. After removing the front rudder, we carried the machine back to camp. We set the machine down a few feet west of the building, and while standing about discussing the last flight, a sudden gust of wind struck the machine and it started to turn it over.

Orville explained that Daniels tried to help but, having no experience in handling such a machine, was knocked down when the machine turned over on him. Orville commented that his escape was miraculous.

After they had lunch and cleared up, Wilbur and Orville walked over to the Kitty Hawk weather station, about 5 miles away, to send a telegram to their father, reaching there at about 3 p.m. As few telegrams were sent from Kitty Hawk, the messages had to be sent to Norfolk where they would be relayed by phone from the weather bureau to the office of one of the telegraph companies. Orville had written out the following message to be sent:

> Success four flights Thursday morning all against twenty-one-mile wind started from level with engine power alone average speed through air thirty-one miles longest 59 seconds inform press home Christmas. Orville Wright.

Joseph Dosher, the weather bureau operator who had a swift connection with Norfolk, told the brothers that the Norfolk operator had asked if he could pass the details on to his reporter friend from the *Norfolk Virginian-Pilot*. The brothers were adamant that they wanted the first

## DID YOU KNOW?

Kites were used during the American Civil War of 1861–65 to deliver letters and newspapers.

news to come from Dayton, and this was relayed back to the Norfolk operator; however, he ignored the message and passed the details on to the reporter. As Orville stated years later, although the report was ninety-nine per cent wrong, at least one fact was correct – there had been a flight! Twenty-one other newspapers over the country also received the news, but only five ordered the story and only three newspapers actually published the account.

It was not until late that evening that the telegram was received at Dayton, but it had significant errors during transmission. This is the wording of the telegram that was sent:

Kitty Hawk N C Dec 17
Bishop M Wright:
7 Hawthorne St
Success four flights Thursday morning all against a twenty one mile wind started from level with engine power alone average speed through air thirty one miles longest 57 seconds inform Press Home Christmas

                      Orevelle Wright

(Note that the 59 seconds on Wilbur's fourth flight had been changed to 57 seconds and Orville's name was misspelled.)

Katharine sent a message to Octave Chanute, who replied with a telegram of congratulations. Milton then asked his son Lorin to prepare a statement for the Associated Press (AP), which he gave to the AP representative at the *Dayton Journal*. Nothing appeared in the *Dayton Journal* the next morning, nor was the Associated Press interested in the story at first. Eventually the next day they sent out a short statement, which was full of inaccuracies and very few of the Associated Press newspapers actually printed it. However, exactly one month later on 17 January, the *New York Herald* had in its magazine a section headed 'The Machine That Flies', complete with an artist's impression of the machine in flight.

>> The brothers (Orville, left, and Wilbur, right) standing by the 1904 Flyer II with a new motor in May 1904 at Huffman Prairie.

## FLYER II, HUFFMAN PRAIRIE, 1904

In early 1904 the brothers asked Charles Taylor if he could take on the day-to-day business of the bicycle shop, allowing them to concentrate on their flight projects. One of the problems they now had was how to keep their work secret against potential rivals, and also to find a field and workshop closer to home instead of the expensive, extended stays at Kitty Hawk. In the spring of 1904 the brothers were given permission to use a meadow 8 miles east of Dayton belonging to Torrance Huffman, a Dayton banker at Huffman Prairie. This time the brothers decided to inform the

Machine on launching track at Huffman Prairie.

press they were about to test the Flyer II, which was very similar in design from the Flyer I.

The first attempt to fly the Flyer II at Huffman Prairie was on 23 May, but despite building a new 100ft-long launch rail for use on low-wind days the winds were not strong enough to take off; therefore, late in the afternoon, Wilbur decided that he would attempt a demonstration run down the track for all the spectators that had arrived. There was difficulty with the engine at first, but after running down the track the machine dropped off the end of the launch rail without taking off.

For the next two days there was heavy rain, but some reporters continued to wait to see if there would be a flight, and were rewarded on 26 May when Orville managed to take-off and fly for 25ft. Milton and some friends were also there to see that flight. The next flight took place on 10 June when Wilbur flew for approximately 60ft. The remainder of the summer was not

▽ Launching track, showing the hangar nearby, at Huffman Prairie.

Orville flying for 356ft at Huffman Prairie on 5 August 1904. A 236ft launch track was used.

very successful, with many flights ending in broken wings, propellers and rudders and only a few short flights. However, on 13 August there were four flights recorded using a 295ft launch track. The first flight by Orville only completed 200ft, but flight two by Wilbur made it to 2,312ft, flight three by Orville to 1,394ft and flight four by Wilbur to 1,558ft – all but flight one went further than their Kitty Hawk record.

On 23 August Orville flew 1,722ft, which was witnessed by Katharine, but the following day Orville was injured when the machine was overturned by a gust of wind. The brothers decided that the only solution to the problem was to construct a catapult launch system,

▲ Wilbur flying at Huffman Prairie in 1904.

which would consist of a 20ft tower with a weight of approximately 1,600lb that would be pulled to the top. A rope would be attached to the weight that ran over pulleys and down the length of the launch rail and then back again to the plane. When the weight dropped, the machine would be pulled along the launch rail for take-off, even in very light winds. Witnessed by Katharine and her friend Harriet Sillman, Wilbur successfully flew 2,001ft on 7 September using the new catapult starting system for the very first time, proving to the brothers that they were now more independent of weather conditions.

From 15 September, the brothers were successful in flying the first half-circle and full-circle. The first complete circle on 20 September was observed by Amos L. Root, the first eyewitness (aside from their mechanic Charles E. Taylor, who was also present) to see the Flyer II in the air. As the editor of the beekeepers trade journal *Gleanings in the Bee Culture*, he was able to write his own eyewitness account of the flight that he called an 'airship' in the 1 January 1905 edition.

The Wright brothers' attempt to market the machines resulted in an officer from the British military establishment visiting the Wrights in Dayton on 24 October 1904. The brothers only showed him the photographs of their flyer and the officer suggested they should tender to the British War Office to sell them a machine that could carry two men at 30mph. With a fairly positive result from the British, the brothers sought the help of their local congressman Robert M. Nevin to assist them approaching the US government,

‹ Orville making two complete circles at Huffman Prairie in 2 minutes 48 seconds and flying a distance of 8,858ft on 7 September 1905.

but due to a misunderstanding when a government department received their letter the Wrights did not get a very positive reply.

For the remainder of the flying season the flights became longer, with the last of the flight season on 9 December, almost a year after the first short flights at Kill Devil Hills. The catapult system had enabled them to extend their time in the air, and allowed them to circle the field five times in 5 minutes.

The Wright brothers were now flying with confidence. The daily accidents still occurred, although fortunately without any serious injury to the pilots. During these periods the brothers found it difficult to maintain complete control and they felt as if the aircraft was almost controlling them, so they tried altering the centre of gravity by moving the engine back, but this made the problem worse and any further attempts to sort the problems were unsuccessful. Any problems concerning the instability of the Flyer II would have to wait until 1905 to be resolved.

## FLYER III, 1905

By January 1905 the brothers were ready to sell their machine and negotiate to those interested, although Wilbur explained to Chanute that they had considered offering the machine to the US first before selling to any foreign

⌃ Start of the first flight of 1905, with Orville at the controls, near the hangar at Huffman Prairie. The two figures in the centre are Wilbur and Charles Taylor. The catapult launching device is seen on the right of the photograph.

▲ Orville flew 12 miles at Huffman Prairie on 29 September 1905 until the fuel was exhausted.

governments. However, in February 1905 the British War Office sent a letter to the Wright brothers asking them to submit terms for the purchase of their aeroplane. The brothers began working on the Flyer III from 23 May, which resulted in extending the canard and front rudder further out for easier control; they also decided that it was essential to the design and for stability in turns to add two vertical vanes called 'blinkers' between the elevators. Within a month Flyer III was ready to start flying trials. The changes to the flying controls included a cradle for the pilot's hips while his hands controlled the two control levers: one for the elevator and one for the rudder.

The first trials of Flyer III began on 23 June when Orville flew 272ft, but his left wing struck the ground while landing and caused some damage to the flyer. In the series of short flights that took place over the next twelve weeks there were accidents each day, but the most serious was on 14 July when the machine, which Orville had only been flying for 12 seconds, started wobbling and then fell to the ground in a nosedive. Orville was thrown out but suffered no injury. This was obviously a concern for the brothers, as safety was the most important issue to them and something about which Wilbur had promised to their father in a letter, but they soon discovered that the solution to the problem was to enlarge the elevator and the machine was back in the air on 24 August.

The next flights were very successful and became quite significant when on 6 September

Orville flying at 60ft, which was higher than the usual secret flights from 1904–05 that were flown between 15–20ft.

Orville flying 1,755ft in 40 seconds on 16 November 1904.

Orville flew four circuits of the field while being airborne for 4 minutes 54 seconds. On 7 September Wilbur flew two complete circuits of the field and was in the air for up to 5 minutes. The distance and time rapidly increased with each flight and on 26 September Wilbur was airborne for 18 minutes 11 seconds, completing sixteen circuits of the field. Orville then contributed to increasing the record to 26 minutes 11 seconds on 3 October and then the following day, with a large

➤ A front view of Orville flying towards the camera. Later that day Wilbur flew twenty-nine times around the field for a distance of 24 miles in 59 minutes 23 seconds. This flight was longer than any of the 105 flights in 1904 and was the last photographed flight of 1905.

group of spectators watching including their father and sister, increased the record further to 33 minutes 17 seconds. The next milestone was on 5 October 1905 when Wilbur was airborne for 59 minutes 23 seconds while flying thirty circles for 24 miles. It was their longest flight to date.

After nine years of trial and error, as well as the risk to their lives, the brothers were now convinced that

>> Wilbur Wright in about 1905 aged 38.

**DID YOU KNOW?**
The brothers only flew together once – on 25 May 1910 in Dayton, Ohio.

not only did they have a practical flying machine but they had also been the first to fly in a controlled, powered, heavier-than-air machine. This gave them the confidence that they were now able to fly for an extended time while under the control of a pilot and be able to land safely. The Wrights made sure that they had witnesses to confirm their flights and also invited reporters so they could spread the word of their achievements. They knew they had created history.

With their trials attracting more and more attention, they became increasingly concerned that observers might steal their ideas before they had patented their machine, so the decision was made

◀◀ Orville Wright in 1905 aged 34.

to stop flying for the time being. Wilbur and Orville had invested a lot of money, time and effort and decided it was now time to recoup some of their expenditure by selling their machine. They were in a difficult position because they knew that even patenting the machine would not protect them from infringements, so they decided to keep the machine secret as long as possible until they had signed contracts. The years 1900–05 had been an adventurous and successful time for the brothers, but it was now time to stop flying and concentrate their efforts on marketing their product – something which would prove much more difficult than they imagined.

★ ★ ★

By 1906 the Wright brothers were challenged by other aviators who were building, flying and selling their own machines and had to make a swift decision whether or not to reduce the price and sell their machine in advance before any of their rivals. The Wright Brothers now had patent No. 821,393 for their flying machine, issued on 22 May 1906, but were to find later that they would have ongoing difficulties relating to patents.

The Wright Brothers did no flying during 1906, but by the winter they started work on developing a new engine. Wilbur's time was also taken up with trying to sell their machines and he sailed for Europe on 16 May 1907 to complete negotiations with Great Britain, France, Italy and Germany. The return trip to New York was aboard RMS *Baltic*, leaving on 16 November and arriving at New York on 22 November. It was then that Wilbur reflected upon what they had achieved over the preceding two years, coming to the conclusion it was time that had not been wasted. They had made important contacts in Britain, France and Germany, but up until that point they still had not sold any aircraft. Wilbur understood that the US Army were now showing serious interest in obtaining a flying machine that could be used for scouting behind enemy lines to observe the area and troop positions, and decided that the winter would be a time to get more machines ready for the spring trade.

**W**ilbur returned to the old camp at Kill Devil Hills on 1 April 1908, only to find very little of it left. Although some walls of the hangar were still standing, the roof had collapsed and there was just a skeleton of the 1902 wing protruding from a small dune east of the old hangar. The Chanute glider had been completely destroyed.

Wilbur employed Oliver O'Neal to assist him in erecting a new building, but progress was slow due to the poor weather and ongoing illness. Charlie Furnas, one of their Dayton mechanics who had said he wanted to learn to fly, arrived at the camp on 15 April and was a great help to Wilbur, and during that time the two of them stayed with the Kill Devil Hills lifesavers.

Once all the accommodation was ready plans were made for the tests to begin. At the time, the newspapers were writing articles about the Wrights' work and as news spread more papers were keen to get involved, with more reporters arriving at Kitty Hawk, which was actually of help to Wilbur because they assisted in moving the aircraft out of the hangar.

The Wrights had not flown since 1905 and they started with a modified Flyer III with two upright seats for pilot and passenger and an improved control system for tests at Kitty Hawk. The new control system had three levers: one for wing warping,

 Camp building at Kitty Hawk in 1908 showing the old building to the left and the newly constructed building on the right.

one for the elevator and one for the rudder. This was their first production aeroplane and became known as the Wright Model A. The first flights were scheduled to take place on 7 May, but due to rain they didn't start until the next morning when they made nine flights – Wilbur made the longest flight when he flew 2,230ft in 59.5 seconds.

On 11 May the brothers completed three flights before 11 a.m.; this time it was Orville who made the best distance and time. On 14 May Wilbur flew with Charlie Furnas aboard, making this the

∧ The condition of the camp when Wilbur arrived there on 10 April 1908. The old 1902 building is on the left and the remains of the 1902 glider can be seen just inside the building.

Wilbur had to leave the camp on 17 May to return to France and deal with some French contracts, leaving Orville to concentrate on getting the military machine ready. Wilbur's aim was for both of them to get involved

first aircraft passenger flight. That afternoon Wilbur had been in the air for 7 minutes when there were problems with the engine, causing it to cut out and the aircraft to crash. It was a complete wreck and Wilbur suffered some quite painful bruises.

## DID YOU KNOW?

**The first mass-produced aeroplane was the Wright Model B, an early pusher biplane the brothers designed in 1910. It had a maximum speed of 40mph.**

▼ Flyer III had two upright seats: one for the pilot and one for a passenger. Three of the lifesaving crew in their white jackets can be seen sitting down on the sand. Taken in 1908, this is thought to be the only photograph of this machine.

L'Aviation en 1908

*I'll tie a string to you next time to keep you from going too high or too far. Its too much trouble to break your records. Will.*

Photo J. Bouveret Le Mans

> Postcard from Wilbur to Orville, sent from France: 'I'll tie a string to you next time to keep you from going too high or too far. It's too much trouble to break your records. Will' (Family Papers Correspondence-Wright Wilbur, September 1908. Wilbur and Orville Wright Manuscript Division, Library of Congress)

in the European and American demonstration flights. It was in the Model A that Wilbur was to circle the Statue of Liberty in New York in 1909 and, as he would be flying over water, a canoe attachment was fitted.

Orville was to leave Kitty Hawk in early May and travel to Washington to inspect the flight-test ground in Fort Myer, Virginia, before returning to Dayton to start work on the military flyer.

◄◄ Wilber examining the canoe attachment before his flight over water.

◄◄ Taking off for their first flight over water.

It was decided that Orville was to undertake the army trials in the USA on his own, with Wilbur warning Orville to be careful in the early practices and do everything slowly. Orville arrived at Fort Myer on 20 August and flew for the first time on 3 September, taking his brother's advice to go slow and easy, flying a circle in 1 minute 11 seconds. On 9 September Orville set three world records – the first was being airborne for 57 minutes 13 seconds, making this a new world endurance record. On his next flight he broke that record when he was airborne for 62 minutes 15 seconds. With his third flight he made their first passenger flight in public while carrying Lieutenant Lahm for 6 minutes 24 seconds, also setting a new endurance record for a flight with a passenger. The records kept coming when on 10 September Orville flew for 65 minutes 52 seconds, breaking his own record yet again, and then once more on 11 September when he flew for 70 minutes 24 seconds.

Chanute arrived on 12 September and observed Orville taking a passenger up and breaking the previous record of a flight with a passenger at 9 minutes 6 seconds. Flying from then until 17 September was restricted due to weather conditions and also because the aircraft was having an overhaul. That was the day Orville was due to fly, taking Lieutenant Thomas Selfridge,

▾ Fort Myer army trials, July 1909.

an officer in the US Signal Corps, as a passenger. Orville had noticed Lieutenant Selfridge carefully inspecting their machine and also asking a lot of questions, which

▼ Orville standing to the right of Fort Myer hanger in July 1909.

concerned Orville because he had discovered that Lieutenant Selfridge was also a member of a group organised by Alexander Graham Bell intending to build a rival aircraft to the Wrights'. Nevertheless, as a member of the official army board making the decision on the suitability of the flyer for the military, the lieutenant was fully entitled to go up as a passenger.

They took off at 5 p.m. and made three circles of the parade ground while keeping a low altitude, but on the third circle Orville climbed to 100ft to enable him to make a wider circle. It was then Orville heard a noise at the rear of the machine, but on looking back he couldn't see anything; however, for safety he cut

◄◄ Wilbur, Orville and Charlie Taylor putting the flyer on to the launch rail, July 1909.

> Orville demonstrates the military flyer at Fort Myer, Virginia in 1909 while Wilbur watches from the ground.

>> Orville and Lieutenant Lahm of the United States Signal Corps making the world's record flight at Fort Myer on 27 July. The aeroplane completed 50 miles at a speed of about 40mph.

the engine and prepared to land as soon as possible. It was already too late: suddenly the aircraft nosedived and crashed into the ground, killing Lieutenant Selfridge and seriously injuring Orville.

While investigating the cause it was found that on 9 September a split had been observed in one of the propellers, which were repaired by Charles Taylor, who had also telegraphed Lorin to send two

▼ Wilbur preparing for a flight in the military flyer at Fort Myer.

replacement blades. These arrived on 16 September and were bolted on, but it was noticed during the investigation that they were 6in longer than the previous blades. However, no blame was attributed to the accident and the army informed Orville that a new contract extension would be issued so they could return the next year to complete their demonstration flights.

▼ Timing the army trials.

I M Cramer, timing the flight.

## DID YOU KNOW?

Orville Wright and J.M.H. Jacobs invented the split-wing flap in 1920. The invention helped to prevent aeroplane stalls and made dive-bombing possible during the First World War.

Wilbur had arrived in Paris on 29 May and was keen to fly by 5 August, but the weather was poor and it was not until 8 August that he made his first flight in Europe when he flew two circuits on the Hunaudiéres racecourse, situated 100 miles from Paris. Wilbur then transferred to Camp d'Auvours, a military base near Le Mans where he was responsible for demonstration flights and also trained pilots. Wilbur was to make significant long-distance flights when on 21 September 1908 he covered 41 miles; he also won the Michelin prize on 31 December with a flight of 90 miles in the time of 2 hours 20 minutes 23 seconds. It was an important time for the Wrights' publicity, and during his stay

<< Wilber and Orville sitting on the steps of the rear porch at 7 Hawthorn Street, Dayton, Ohio.

Wilbur had carried approximately forty passengers, combined with further demonstrations in front of many distinguished VIPs and royalty.

Wilbur moved to Pau (south of France), where he made sixty-four flights. During his time in Pau, Wilbur was joined by Orville, who was still recovering from his flying accident, and his sister Katharine. Wilbur's demonstrations in Europe were hugely successful, and it was the French who were the first to acknowledge the Wright brothers' accomplishment for inventing flight, honouring them with the prestigious Legion of Honour five years after their first flight in 1903.

When they returned to the USA after a successful tour of Europe there was much celebration and they were presented with gold medals awarded by President Taft of the Aero Club of America. However, although the medals displayed the busts of the brothers, their aircraft and the dates of the first flight made by Orville at Fort Myer and Wilbur in France, there was no

▼ Wright Company factory, Dayton, Ohio.

inscription of the date 17 December 1903 recognising that the Wright Brothers were the inventors of flight.

In the final demonstration for the army, Orville had to complete a number of tests. He flew on his own for 1 hour 20 minutes, and with a passenger on another flight for 1 hour 12 minutes on a 10-mile round trip. The official average speed checked was 42.583mph – 2.583mph over the set contract time of 40mph. The purchase price for the aircraft was $25,000, but with a contractual addition of $2,500 for each mile over the 42mph, arriving at a total of $30,000.

On 22 November 1909 the Wright Company was formed, with Wilbur as president and Orville Wright and Andrew Freedman (an American businessman who served on the board of directors) as vice-presidents. The brothers hoped that now the board of directors and company management would deal with the business side, leaving them to return to their aviation research. However, it was not long before problems arose when the brothers attempted to establish themselves as inventors of the aeroplane, and to defend themselves from those keen to profit at their expense. The patent courts in America and Europe became involved and Wilbur took on much of the legal burden, although Orville did help a little.

From 1909-10 the brothers worked on their next model, known as the 'Transitional Model A'. This was their first machine with the elevator at the back whilst still retaining the canard in the front to control the pitch of the aircraft. The 'Transitional Model A' was considered the aircraft between the models A and B and was used for training civilian pilots from Simms Station at Huffman Prairie.

In January 1910 the Wrights set up their factory at Dayton, a flying school at Simms Station and a civilian flying school at Montgomery, Alabama. Orville was kept busy teaching students to fly at Simms Station, including training 119 army and navy officers between 1910 and 1916. One of his pupils was Canadian pilot Captain Arthur 'Roy' Brown, who later flew for the RAF during the First World War and was involved in the shooting down of the infamous German fighter pilot Baron Manfred von Richthofen.

On 21 May 1910 Wilbur made his last flight at Simms Station and just four days later Orville flew with Wilbur as a passenger. This was the first and only time they flew together and was also the same day that their father made his first flight.

The new Wright Model B dispensed with the canard and had an elevator behind the larger twin rudder at the back of the aircraft. It was also significant because the first experiments began in wheeled

‹ Photograph from a series of flights from May through to July after the opening of the Wright Flying School in 1910.

⌃ Distant view of Bishop Milton Wright during his first ride in an aeroplane (the transitional model, otherwise known as the A–B, used to train civilian pilots), flying at 350ft over Simms Station, 1910. It was also the first and last flight that Wilbur and Orville had together.

⌃ The single elevator at the back behind the twin rudder can be clearly seen on the Wright Model B.

landing gear when wheels were fitted to the skids but still used wing warping to control the roll.

Also in 1910 the 'Baby Wright', also called the 'Roadster' – a small single-seat racing machine that could achieve speeds of up to 80mph – appeared. It was built for the Wright brothers' English friend, pilot Alec Ogilvie, who flew in the Gordon Bennett race in 1910, coming third. The Wright brothers entered their own Model R, named the 'Baby Grand', into the race but one of their pilots, Walter Brookins, suffered engine failure in a test flight and crashed. The damage to the aircraft was severe and it was unable to take part in the race. After later being rebuilt it was flown on

exhibition flights. Another exhibition model was the Model EX, which followed on from the Model R and was the first aircraft to be flown across America by pilot Cal Rodgers. Between 1912 and 1913 two further aircraft appeared: the Model C and Model D. The Model C

A large crowd of spectators gathered at the edge of a field at Simms Station watching the flights on 18 May 1910. This particular flight was the glider test of the automatic stabiliser.

was to replace the Model B and the Model D was a fast single-seat 'speed scout' built for the US Army.

## THE AUTOMATIC STABILISER

Orville and Wilbur had planned to return to Kitty Hawk to test their automatic stabiliser, which could fly the aeroplane straight without a pilot's intervention on a new glider, but Wilbur was unable to go due to tiredness from a lot of travelling, so Orville went with his brother Lorin, nephew Horace and Alec Ogilvie. When they arrived at the old camp on 10 October 1911 they saw parts of the 1905–08 machines poking out of the sand. For the first week they

▲ The Wright Model B on the starting track in 1909. Note the triangular blinkers mounted on the forward skid struts.

◄◄ The Wright Model B had wheeled landing gear and two upright seats for the pilot and one passenger. Model B was the first mass-produced aeroplane, and the first without a canard. It had a single elevator at the back, which was located behind the twin rudder.

▶▶ View of the glider in flight at Kitty Hawk in 1911. These gliding experiments were carried out with a glider resembling the 1911 powered machine, although it had no engine.

▼ View of the glider in front of the camp building at Kitty Hawk in 1911.

flew kites on the beach and then Orville and Alec started gliding. There were certainly accidents over the next few months, but nothing serious. Orville made thirty-one flights and on 24 October he set the world's first soaring record when he remained airborne for 9 minutes and 45 seconds.

The Wright Model E became the test machine for the automatic stabiliser and on 31 December 1913 Orville took off at the Huffman Prairie field to demonstrate in front of the Aero Club judges. He flew seven circuits of the field with his hands above his head, winning the 1913 Collier Trophy from the Aero Club of America for that achievement.

## DID YOU KNOW?

US astronaut Neil Armstrong carried a piece of muslin and a piece of wood from the 1903 flyer when he stepped on the moon in 1969.

▲ Glider at Kitty Hawk, 1911.

▲ Glider being prepared for flight by Orville and his assistants; a number of reporters stand off to the right, 1911.

≫ Group photograph in front of the glider at Kill Devil Hills in 1911. Sitting, left–right: Tom Tate, Orville Wright and Alexander Ogilvie; standing: Lorin Wright and a group of journalists, including Van Ness Harwood of the *New York World*, Berges of the American News Service, Arnold Kruckman of the *New York American*, Mitchell of the *New York Herald* and John Mitchell of the Associated Press.

◄◄ Rear view of the glider in flight at Kitty Hawk, 1911.

◄ The tower (derrick) with the 1,600lb weight being pulled up to the top ready to drop and pull the flyer along the launch rail for take-off.

## DID YOU KNOW?

17 December is Wright Brothers Day in the USA, commemorating the first flight in an heavier-than-air, mechanically propelled aeroplane.

❯ Model A machine on launch track. The wing support to keep the flyer upright when on the ground can be seen under the right wing.

◄ Machine taking off.

> A forward view of
the aircraft coming
in to land.

# WILBUR DIES FROM TYPHOID FEVER

The brothers had purchased some land in the exclusive suburb of Oakwood, Dayton, in 1911 with a view to having their own mansion built. They were still living at 7 Hawthorn Street and would move into the mansion after it was built, but sadly Wilbur, who was 45 in the spring of 1912, became ill, his illness no doubt worsened by constant travelling and the stress of the number of lawsuits he was dealing with. On 2 May 1912 Wilbur, Orville, Katharine and their father Milton went on a picnic. Whilst there Wilbur, who had just returned from a trip to Boston, complained that he thought he was developing a fever; his doctor confirmed that he had typhoid. Wilbur died on 30 May 1912 with his family around him.

▲ The Wright brothers' house, which originally stood in Dayton, Ohio, but was later moved to Greenfield Village in Dearborn, Michigan. (Courtesy of Andrew Balet, via Wikimedia Commons)

**M**ilton, Orville and Katharine continued to live at 7 Hawthorn Street until 1913 when they moved into the newly built mansion. Milton maintained a fairly active life and enjoyed meeting the many visitors to the house until he passed away on 3 April 1917 at the age of 88.

After the death of his brother, Orville became president of the Wright Company. In 1915 he decided to sell the company and open his own aeronautical research laboratory, where he was involved in scientific research for the rest of his life. The Wright Company then merged with the Glenn L. Martin Company to form the Wright–Martin Company.

The Wright Aeronautical Company, New Jersey, was the successor to the Wright–Martin Company from 1919 and built aircraft and aircraft engines until 1929, when it merged with Curtiss to form Curtiss–Wright. Orville continued to be heavily involved in aviation matters, and in 1920 President Woodrow Wilson appointed him to the National Advisory Committee for Aeronautics, where he served for twenty-eight years. In March 1917 Orville found a St Bernard puppy in the baggage room at Dayton railroad station whom he named Scipio. He was very fond of Scipio and when Orville died in 1948 he was still carrying a photograph of the St Bernard in his wallet.

▲ Front view of Hawthorn Hill in winter, Dayton, Ohio.

> Orville with Scipio, his beloved St Bernard.

>> Group picture in the side porch of Orville's home of Orville (standing behind Katharine), Milton (seated in the centre next to Katharine) and their friends and family – Earl N. Findley, nephew Horace Wright, John R. McMahon and Pliny Williamson.

Orville had many visitors to Dayton, including Colonel Charles Lindberg, the first man to fly solo across the Atlantic, and Amelia Earhart, who was the first woman to do so.

The 1903 Flyer I, which only flew on 17 December 1903 before being stored in a shed at their Dayton home, was refurbished by Orville in 1916 for an exhibition at the Massachusetts Institute of Technology, and in January 1928 it was shipped to the Science Museum, London, where it was displayed for almost twenty years. It returned to the US and was displayed in the Smithsonian Museum from 1945, and in 1976 it was transferred to the National Air and Space Museum in Washington.

▲ Group picture, including Orville, Milton and Katharine in 1915.

▲ Major John F. Curry (in the centre, holding a walking stick) and Colonel Charles Lindbergh to his right (Orville is to the left of Major Curry), who came to pay Orville a personal call at Wright Field, Dayton, Ohio on 22 June 1927. Major Curry had learned to fly in 1915 and became the first National Commander of the Civil Air Patrol, the United States Air Force Auxiliary 1941.

◄ Orville taking his sister Katharine up for a flight in the Wright Model HS in 1915.

Orville continued with his research until 30 January 1948 when he suffered a heart attack and died three days later.

▾ Underside view of the Wright brothers' reconstructed 1903 motor.

▲ Left front side of the 1903 motor. It weighed 200lb fully fuelled and produced over 12hp.

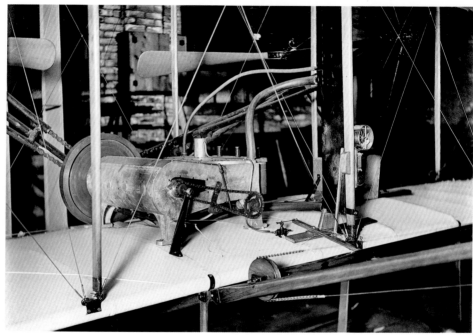

⌃ Rear view of the Wright brothers' 1903 motor in the shop, 1 January 1928, before its shipment to the Science Museum in London.

# GLOSSARY

**aerodynamics:** the study of the motion of air and the forces on bodies moving through the air.

**aerofoil:** a structure with curved surfaces designed to give the most favourable ratio of lift to drag in flight.

**aileron:** two moveable flaps on the wings of an aircraft that can be moved up or down to cause the aircraft to bank or roll.

**anemometer:** instrument to measure speed of wind.

**bank:** a flight manoeuvre in which one wing points toward the ground and the other to the sky.

**barometer:** an instrument to measure pressure of the atmosphere.

**biplane:** a fixed-wing aircraft with two main wings stacked one above the other.

**canard:** an aircraft whose horizontal stabilising surfaces are forward of the main wing, sometimes replacing the tail.

**drag:** the force that works against thrust and is caused by air resistance. Smooth surfaces have less drag than rough surfaces.

**elevators:** a movable, horizontal aerofoil, usually attached to the horizontal stabiliser on the tail that is used to control pitch.

**engine:** part of the aeroplane that provides power to pull or push the plane through the air.

**fin:** a vertical attachment to the tail of an aircraft, providing directional stability.

**flaps:** hinged aerofoils that are normally located at the trailing edge of the wing.

**fuselage:** the main streamlined body of an aeroplane to which the wings and tail are fixed.

**gear:** the landing wheels or floats that support an aeroplane on land or water.

**glider:** a fixed-wing, heavier-than-air aircraft without an engine for thrust.

**lateral axis (pitch):** the pitch axis passes through the plane from wingtip to wingtip. Pitch moves the aircraft's nose up and down. The elevators are the primary control of pitch.

**lift:** an upward force caused by the rush of air over the wings and supporting the aeroplane in flight.

**longitudinal axis (roll):** the rotation of an aircraft about its longitudinal axis that passes through the plane from nose to tail. The ailerons are the main control of bank but the rudder also has an effect on bank. An aircraft is turned by controlling the roll and yaw.

**monoplane:** an aeroplane with one set of wings.

**propeller:** an aerofoil that the engine turns to provide the thrust, pulling the aeroplane through the air.

**pusher configuration:** where the propeller shaft faces the rear of the aircraft and thrust is produced by the propeller pushing the aircraft, rather than pulling it.

**rudder:** control surface hinged to the back of the vertical fin.

**stall:** reduction of speed to the point where the wing stops producing lift.

**tail:** part of the aeroplane to which the rudder and elevators are attached.

**thrust:** forward force caused by the engine powering the propeller.

**tractor configuration:** an aircraft that has the engine mounted with the propeller in front of it so that it is 'pulled' through the air.

**triplane:** a fixed-wing aircraft with three vertically stacked main wings.

**velocity:** speed through the air.

**vertical axis (yaw):** flight condition of an aircraft in which it rotates about its vertical axis. Yaw moves the nose of the aircraft from side to side. The rudder is the main control of yaw.

**weight and balance:** distribution of weight in an aircraft and the location of its centre of gravity. The centre of gravity is the point where the weight is balanced.

**wind tunnel:** tubular structures in which high-speed movements of air are produced to test models of aircraft and aerofoils to the airflow around them and the aerodynamic forces acting upon them.

**wings:** part of the aeroplane designed to provide the lift force to oppose the weight force.

# BIBLIOGRAPHY

Abzug, Malcolm J. and Larrabee, Eugene E., *Airplane Stability and Control* (Cambridge University Press, 1997).

Allen, C.B., *The Concept of Flight that Worked*, Bee-Hive, January (United Aircraft Corporation, 1953).

Burton, Walt and Findsen, Owen, *The Wright Brothers Legacy* (Harry N. Abrams, 2003).

Crouch, Tom, *The Bishop's Boys: The Life of Wilbur and Orville Wright* (W.W. Norton & Co., 1989).

Harrison, Michael, *Airborne at Kitty Hawk* (Cassell and Company Ltd, 1953).

Haven, Gil, *The Wrights at the Stick*, Bee-Hive, January (United Aircraft Corporation, 1953).

Kelly, Fred C., *The Wright Brothers: A Biography Authorized by Orville Wright* (Aviators Bookshelf) (Bantam Doubleday Dell Publishing, 1984)

McCullough, David, *The Wright Brothers* (Simon & Schuster, 2015).

McSurely, Alexander, *The Horsepower at Kitty Hawk*, Bee-Hive, January (United Aircraft Corporation, 1953).

Renstrom, Arthur George, *Wilbur and Orville Wright*, Monographs in Aerospace History, No. 32 (NASA, September 2003).

Walsh, John Evangelist, *First Flight: The Untold Story of the Wright Brothers* (George Allen & Unwin Ltd, 1976).